BELGICA

GAULISH VILLAGE

COMPENDIUM

LAUDANUM

AQUARIUM

TOTORUM

LUTETIA

SPQR

ARMORICA

GAUL
(ROMAN CONQUEST)
50 BC

CELTICA

AQUITANIA

PROVINCIA

THE YEAR IS 50 BC. GAUL IS ENTIRELY OCCUPIED BY THE
ROMANS. WELL, NOT ENTIRELY . . . ONE SMALL VILLAGE OF
THE INDOMITABLE GAULS STILL HOLDS OUT AGAINST THE
INVADERS. AND LIFE IS NOT EASY FOR THE ROMAN LEGION-
ARIES WHO GARRISON THE FORTIFIED CAMPS OF TOTORUM,
AQUARIUM, LAUDANUM AND COMPENDIUM . . .

ASTERIX, THE HERO OF THESE ADVENTURES. A SHREWD, CUNNING LITTLE WARRIOR, ALL PERILOUS MISSIONS ARE IMMEDIATELY ENTRUSTED TO HIM. ASTERIX GETS HIS SUPERHUMAN STRENGTH FROM THE MAGIC POTION BREWED BY THE DRUID GETAFIX . . .

OBELIX, ASTERIX'S INSEPARABLE FRIEND. A MENHIR DELIVERY-MAN BY TRADE, ADDICTED TO WILD BOAR. OBELIX IS ALWAYS READY TO DROP EVERYTHING AND GO OFF ON A NEW ADVENTURE WITH ASTERIX – SO LONG AS THERE'S WILD BOAR TO EAT, AND PLENTY OF FIGHTING. HIS CONSTANT COMPANION IS DOGMATIX, THE ONLY KNOWN CANINE ECOLOGIST, WHO HOWLS WITH DESPAIR WHEN A TREE IS CUT DOWN.

GETAFIX, THE VENERABLE VILLAGE DRUID, GATHERS MISTLETOE AND BREWS MAGIC POTIONS. HIS SPECIALITY IS THE POTION WHICH GIVES THE DRINKER SUPERHUMAN STRENGTH. BUT GETAFIX ALSO HAS OTHER RECIPES UP HIS SLEEVE . . .

CACOFONIX, THE BARD. OPINION IS DIVIDED AS TO HIS MUSICAL GIFTS. CACOFONIX THINKS HE'S A GENIUS. EVERY-ONE ELSE THINKS HE'S UNSPEAKABLE. BUT SO LONG AS HE DOESN'T SPEAK, LET ALONE SING, EVERYBODY LIKES HIM . . .

FINALLY, VITALSTATISTIX, THE CHIEF OF THE TRIBE. MAJESTIC, BRAVE AND HOT-TEMPERED, THE OLD WARRIOR IS RESPECTED BY HIS MEN AND FEARED BY HIS ENEMIES. VITALSTATISTIX HIMSELF HAS ONLY ONE FEAR, HE IS AFRAID THE SKY MAY FALL ON HIS HEAD TOMORROW. BUT AS HE ALWAYS SAYS, TOMORROW NEVER COMES.

GOSCINNY AND UDERZO

PRESENT
An Asterix Adventure

STERIX
OBELIX
AT SEA

by ALBERT UDERZO

and DEREK HOCKRIDGE

ORION

To my grandson, Thomas,
and in homage to that great actor,
Kirk Douglas

Original title: *La Galère d'Obélix*

Original edition © 1996 Les Éditions Albert René / Goscinny-Uderzo
English translation: © 1996 Les Éditions Albert René / Goscinny-Uderzo

Fifth impression: August 2003

Exclusive Licensee: Orion Publishing Group
Translators: Anthea Bell and Derek Hockridge
Lettering and text layout: Bryony Newhouse

First published in Great Britain in 1996 by Hodder Headline plc

This edition first published in 2002 by
Orion Books Ltd
Orion House, 5 Upper St Martin's Lane,
London WC2H 9EA

Printed in Italy
www.asterix.tm.fr

A CIP catalogue record for this book is available
from the British Library

ISBN 0 75284 717 1 (cased)
ISBN 0 75284 778 3 (paperback)

Distributed in the United States of America
by Sterling Publishing Co., Inc.
387 Park Avenue South, New York,
NY 10016-8810

5

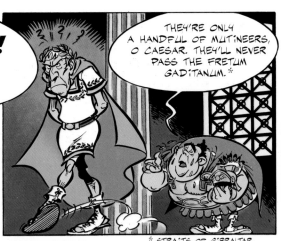

* STRAITS OF GIBRALTAR.

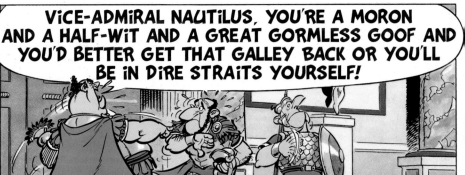

7

YOU'D LIKE THE WAY AFRIC'S SUNNY FOUNTAINS ROLL DOWN THEIR GOLDEN SAND!

HISPANIA'S THE PLACE! IT'S SPAIN-FULLY OBVIOUS!

WE'D FIND A BETTER PORT IN LUSITANIA.

HUH!

EVEN IF CAESAR PURSUED US TO BELGICA, HE MIGHT MEET HIS WATERLOO THERE!

♪ HEIM, HEIM... THERE'S NO PLACE LIKE HEIM! ♪

LISTEN, WE HAVE TO TAKE REFUGE SOMEWHERE THERE ARE NO ROMANS! BUT AS WE ALL KNOW, THE ROMANS ARE EVERYWHERE!

I SAY, I'VE JUST HAD A BRAINWAVE, OLD FRUIT!

4A

MY UNCLE ANTICLIMAX* IN BRITAIN TOLD ME ABOUT SOME INDOMITABLE GAULS IN AN ARMORICAN VILLAGE WHO KNOCK THE ROMANS FOR SIX WITH A MAGIC POTION! JOLLY GOOD WHEEZE, WHAT?

JOIN THE LEGIONS THEY SAID... IT'S A MANS LIFE IN THE LEGIONS...

?!

* SEE ASTERIX IN BRITAIN

IF THAT'S SO, THEN LET'S MAKE FOR THIS GAULISH VILLAGE! EVERYONE AGREE?

CLICK!

WE AGREE!!!

AND SO CAESAR'S MAGNIFICENT GALLEY CHANGES COURSE AND SETS OFF FOR ARMORICA TO TAKE REFUGE WITH THE INDOMITABLE GAULS.

4B

LATER, SOME WAY OFF IN GAUL...

I HAD A TERRIBLE NIGHTMARE LAST NIGHT, ASTERIX!

YOU DID?

I DREAMED THAT JULIUS CAESAR DECIDED TO WITHDRAW ALL THE GARRISONS SURROUNDING THE VILLAGE!

JUST A TOUCH OF INDIGESTION, OBELIX! I KEEP TELLING YOU NOT TO EAT MORE THAN THREE BOARS BEFORE GOING TO BED!

BUT I CAN'T GET TO SLEEP WITHOUT AT LEAST FOUR INSIDE ME!

WELL, IT WAS ONLY A NIGHTMARE! AND EVEN IF YOUR DREAM CAME TRUE...

WHAT DO YOU MEAN, CAME TRUE?!

WHY NOT? WE MIGHT FINALLY GET PEACE WITH HONOUR!

COME ALONG, DOGMATIX! WE WANT NOTHING TO DO WITH THESE POLICIES OF APPEASEMENT!

?!

OH, OBELIX, DON'T BE SO SILLY! I WAS ONLY JOKING!

OH NO, YOU WEREN'T, MISTER ASTERIX!

YOU WERE INSULTING THE MEMORY OF VERCINGETORIX!

HAVE YOU GONE COMPLETELY BONKERS?

RAISE THE ALARM!! THE ROMANS ARE ABOUT TO ATTACK!!

!!!

A GOOD THING THE ROMANS HAVE GOT MORE SENSE THAN YOU, MISTER ASTERIX!

THAT'S FUNNY! THERE WAS NOTHING TO SUGGEST THEY WERE GOING TO ATTACK!

9

I SAW THEM! THE GARRISONS OF ALL FOUR FORTIFIED CAMPS ARE DRAWN UP ON THE OTHER SIDE OF THE FOREST!

!!?

HMMM..

RIGHT! WE MUST BE PREPARED! CAN YOU DOLE OUT THE MAGIC POTION, GETAFIX?

I MADE TWO CAULDRONS JUST IN CASE, ALTHOUGH ONE IS PLENTY!

HURRY UP! NEXT!

THE EFFECTS OF THE POTION NEVER CEASE TO AMAZE ME!

SOMETHING WRONG, OBELIX?

POOR OLD OBELIX! I EXPECT GETAFIX WOULDN'T GIVE HIM ANY MAGIC POTION, AS USUAL!

WE KNOW IT HAD A PERMANENT EFFECT ON HIM... BUT WHAT WOULD HAPPEN IF HE DRANK SOME MORE NOW?

THERE'D BE DANGEROUS SIDE EFFECTS, ASTERIX, AND ALL MY SKILL WOULD BE POWERLESS TO COUNTERACT THEM!

SOON AFTERWARDS...

THIS IS ODD, O DRUID! OBELIX IS MISSING!

YOU KNOW HOW TOUCHY HE IS! HE MUST HAVE GONE OFF IN A SULK, BUT I'M SURE HE'LL BE THE FIRST TO GO FOR THE ROMANS.

AS IT HAPPENS, THE ROMANS ARE NOT FAR AWAY. THE FOUR GARRISONS ARE DRAWN UP ON PARADE, BEING REVIEWED BY THEIR NEW COMMANDER, VICE-ADMIRAL NAUTILUS.

ANOTHER BRASS HAT SENT OUT FROM ROME!

LOOKS LIKE HE'LL HAVE THE BRASS TO MAKE US FIGHT THOSE GAULS!

LEGIONARIES, I'M HERE TO PUT SOME BACKBONE INTO YOU! DISCIPLINE IS THE STRENGTH OF THE ROMAN ARMY!

AND FOR A START...

STAND TO **ATTENTION!**

YOU DO JUST THAT. BECAUSE WE'RE GOING TO ATTEND TO YOU, ROMANS!

?!

WHOOOSH!

TELL ME, ROMAN, WHY THIS FULL-SCALE ATTACK?

BUT... BUT WE WERE ONLY REHEARSING THE PARADE TO WELCOME ADMIRAL CRUSTACIUS!

THEN TELL YOUR ADMIRAL CRUSTIFERUS THAT IF THERE'S ANY PARADING AROUND HERE...

...WE DO IT!

PAF!

LATER, AFTER GATHERING HERBS IN THE FOREST, THE DRUID RETURNS TO HIS HUT.

POOR OLD OBELIX!

THIS IS DREADFUL!

APPALLING!

BANG! BANG! BANG!

WHAT ON EARTH ...?!

BANG! BANG!

SURELY THEY'D NEVER DARE...

IT'S THE ONLY WAY TO GET HIM OUT!

PHEW!

BANG!

A GOOD THING WE'RE STILL FEELING THE EFFECTS OF THE MAGIC POTION!

SO IS HE, IT SEEMS!

BANG! BANG!

RIGHT, EVERYBODY OUT! ASTERIX WILL SIT UP WITH HIM ALONE, WHILE I TRY TO MAKE AN ANTIDOTE.

OH, OBELIX, YOU STUPID IDIOT! WHY DID YOU IGNORE GETAFIX'S WISE ADVICE? WHAT'S TO BECOME OF DOGMATIX AND ME IF YOU STAY STONY AS A MENHIR FOR EVER?

14

NIGHT HAS FALLEN ON THE LITTLE VILLAGE. EVERYONE IS DEEPLY UPSET BY THE INCIDENT. LIGHT SHOWS IN ONLY TWO HUTS...

ONE IS THE HOME OF THE DRUID, WHO IS NOT VERY HOPEFULLY BREWING A POTION WHICH HE ALONE KNOWS THE SECRET...

AND THE OTHER IS POOR OBELIX'S HOUSE. HIS FRIEND ASTERIX IS STILL SITTING UP WITH HIM.

IN THE SMALL HOURS...

HAS HE MOVED AT ALL?

I'M AFRAID NOT.

NOW TO WAIT FOR THE POTION TO TAKE EFFECT... AND HOPE!

AREN'T YOU SURE IT WILL WORK, THEN?

I'VE NEVER HAD A CASE LIKE THIS BEFORE... BUT WE MUST LEAVE NO STONE UNTURNED!

YOU'RE THE BEST DRUID IN THE UNIVERSE, GETAFIX! DOGMATIX AND I ARE SURE YOU'LL MANAGE TO CURE OBELIX!

WOOF!

MAY TOUTATIS HEAR YOU, ASTERIX! MAY TOUTATIS HEAR YOU!

HERE'S THE ADMIRAL, VICE-ADMIRAL!

ANOTHER OF THE TOP BRASS!

YOU CALL THESE ROMANS? GONE INTO A DECLINE ALREADY, HAVE THEY???

ER... WELL, THE FACT IS...

THE FACT IS WHAT, NAUTILUS?

WELL, YOU SEE, WE WERE JUST PEACEFULLY PARADING...

...WHEN ALL OF A SUDDEN...

ARE YOU SAYING THAT HANDFUL OF GAULS DID THIS TO YOU?

WELL, THEY ARE A HANDFUL... I WAS MUCH STRUCK BY IT MYSELF, ADMIRAL!

NEVER MIND! FOLLOW ME. I HAVE TO TALK TO YOU.

WELL, ADMIRAL CRUSTACIUS, CAN YOU TELL ME WHAT WE'RE DOING IN THIS JUPITER-FORSAKEN COUNTRY?

OUR FLEET IS FOLLOWING CAESAR'S GALLEY AT A DISTANCE. IT IS NOW APPROACHING THE COAST OF ARMORICA, AND OBVIOUSLY THE MUTINEERS WILL TRY TO TAKE REFUGE IN THE VILLAGE OF INDOMITABLE GAULS!

I GET IT! AS SOON AS THEY DISEMBARK AND LEAVE THE SHIP, WE GRAB IT BACK! BRILLIANT IDEA!!!

HO, HO, HO! AND I'LL SOON PERSUADE THE GAULS TO HAND THOSE MUTINEERS OVER!

ER... THAT MIGHT NOT BE SUCH A BRILLIANT IDEA!

THERE'S THE SIGNAL, ADMIRAL!

THAT'S QUITE SOME SIGNAL!

JUST AS I EXPECTED! NOW TO MAKE OFF WITH CAESAR'S GALLEY ON THE QUIET, WITHOUT ROUSING THOSE GAULS!

...SO WE THOUGHT YOU MIGHT LET US STAY HERE UNTIL THE ROMANS FORGET ABOUT US!

YOU CAME TO THE RIGHT PLACE, SPARTAKIS, FOR...

...FOR STRONG IN OUR PROFOUND SENSE OF DUTY, WE OWE IT TO OURSELVES TO WELCOME THE OPPRESSED, THE MARTYRS AND ORPHANS OF A DEFEATED LAND, CRUSHED UNDERFOOT BY THE CALIGAE OF THE ROMAN L...

...EGIONS!

!?

PAF!

NOW I DON'T NEED ANYONE ELSE... OOMPH!... TO MAKE ME LOOK RIDICULOUS!

YOU SAY YOU HOPPED IT IN CAESAR'S OWN GALLEY?

THAT'S RIGHT! HE MUST BE HOPPING MAD!

QUICK! WE MUST ROUSE THE VILLAGE. I'LL DOLE OUT MORE MAGIC POTION!

SO ISN'T ANYONE GOING TO HELP ME UP? I MEAN, I AM YOUR CHIEF, YOU KNOW!!!

QUICK, ASTERIX! THE DRUID'S HANDING OUT MAGIC POTION.

WHAT, AGAIN? WHAT FOR?

TO GET CAESAR'S GALLEY STOWED AWAY!

CAESAR'S WHAT?

FUNNY SORT OF CUSTOM. DRINKING SOUP BEFORE YOU LEAVE YOUR VILLAGE. WHAT'S IT FOR?

YOU'LL SOON FIND OUT!

BY POSEIDON, WHAT A MIRACLE!

BY NEPTUNE, WHAT A CHEEK!!

I SAY, OLD BOY, THIS GAULISH VILLAGE IS A BIT OF LUCK, WHAT?

I FEEL QUITE CARRIED AWAY!

QUICK! WE MUST LOSE NO TIME IN WARNING ADMIRAL CRUSTACIUS!

SOON AFTERWARDS...

AVE, ADMIRAL CRUSTACIUS! YOU WERE RIGHT AS USUAL. THE MUTINEERS DID COME ASHORE NEAR THE GAULISH VILLAGE... BUT THE GAULS HAVE TAKEN CAESAR'S GALLEY INTO THE VILLAGE FOR SAFE KEEPING!

BY ALL THE GODS OF HADES!!! I HOPE YOU TOOK CARE TO ANCHOR YOUR OWN SHIP WHERE THOSE SAVAGES CAN'T GET AT IT!

IT WENT UP IN FLAMES AS PRE-ARRANGED FOR THE SIGNAL, O ADMIRAL!

GNGNGN!

I DO HOPE YOU ENJOY THE CIRCUS, CAPTAIN!

FLAP!
FLAP!
FLAP!
FLAP!

ISN'T HE JUST DARLING? YOU MUST BE NEW HERE! WHAT'S YOUR NAME? THIS WAY, SWEETIE-PIE!

DON'T WANT TO!

FUNNY THING... YOU REMIND ME OF POOR OBELIX! NOTHING LIKE AS FAT, OF COURSE!

IN THE FIRST PLACE HE IS **NOT** FAT, JUST WELL-COVERED!

AND NOW WE'LL TAKE THAT LITTLE TOWEL OFF SO I CAN MEASURE YOUR DEAR LITTLE TUMMY!

DON'T WANT TO!

LATER...

HE MUST BE RELATED TO OBELIX! THERE'S SUCH A FAMILY LIKENESS I THOUGHT IT WOULD BE FUN TO MAKE HIM STRIPED BREECHES TOO!

YOU NEVER GAVE ME TIME TO EXPLAIN! THIS LITTLE BOY **IS** OBELIX, UNDER THE EFFECTS OF ONE OF OUR DRUID'S POTIONS!

THUD!

GUTTERSNIPES!!! SCAMPS! YOU LITTLE IMPS!!!

19 A

HERE ARE SOME ROAST BOARS TO TAKE YOUR MIND OFF YOUR TROUBLES, OBELIX!

THERE ARE STILL TWO LEFT, YOU KNOW. YOU DID ASK FOR THREE!

I... I'M NOT HUNGRY ANY MORE!

BOOHOOOHOOOOOOOOO

I'M FINISHED! I CAN'T EVEN EAT THREE BOARS AT A SITTING!

POOR LITTLE OBELIX! I HEARD WHAT HAPPENED TO YOU! NEVER MIND, IT'S NOT SO BAD!

SMACK

THERE! FEELING BETTER NOW?

WGHSTRFG!

HUH!

19 B

23

24

DOGMATIX IS BEHAVING ODDLY! THAT MEANS OBELIX MUST BE IN DANGER!!!!

WOOF! WOOF!

YOU WAIT HERE, DOGMATIX. I MUST TELL THE OTHERS!

OBELIX IS IN DANGER!! I'M OFF TO HELP HIM!

THIS MUST BE THE ROMANS' DOING! WE'LL BE WITH YOU, ASTERIX!

WAIT WHILE I MAKE ANOTHER CAULDRON OF POTION! I THINK YOU'RE GOING TO NEED SOME MORE!

SOON AFTERWARDS...

YOU WILL BE AMONG THE FEW VISITORS TO OUR VILLAGE EVER TO HAVE DRUNK THE MAGIC POTION!

IT'S A GREAT HONOUR FOR US, O VENERABLE DRUID!

AND FINALLY...

DOGMATIX WILL LEAD US STRAIGHT TO OBELIX'S KIDNAPPERS!

SNIFF! SNIFF! SNIFF!

I KNEW IT! THAT'S WHERE OBELIX IS BEING HELD PRISONER!

SURE ENOUGH, THE ADMIRAL'S SHIP, ALL SAILS SET, IS MAKING FOR OSTIA, THE PORT OF ROME, WITH A POOR LITTLE GAUL BELOW DECKS AND FEELING VERY LOW...

SO I GO BACK TO CHILDHOOD! SO I LOSE MY STRENGTH! THE ROMANS AREN'T AFRAID OF ME ANY MORE AND I'M THEIR PRISONER...

OH ASTERIX, PLEASE COME AND HELP ME OUT OF THIS!

WHAT ARE WE WAITING FOR? WE MUST CATCH UP WITH THE ROMAN SHIP AND RESCUE OBELIX!

MY CREW AND I ARE READY TO PURSUE THE ADMIRAL'S GALLEY, ASTERIX!

I'LL COME WITH YOU. I'VE JUST HAD AN IDEA WHICH MIGHT SOLVE POOR OBELIX'S PROBLEMS!

?!

HERE'S YOUR GOURD OF POTION, ASTERIX! I'VE FILLED THIS BARREL TOO, BECAUSE I WON'T BE ABLE TO BREW ANY MORE ON THE VOYAGE!

WE'LL KEEP IT AWAY FROM THE BARRELS OF DRINKING WATER, TO BE ON THE SAFE SIDE!

AND SOON AFTERWARDS...

WE'LL SOON OVER-TAKE THE ADMIRAL'S SHIP, THANKS TO THE EFFECTS OF YOUR POTION, O DRUID!

YES, AND ONCE WE'VE RESCUED OBELIX I'LL TELL YOU MY IDEA, ASTERIX!

FLOP! FLOP! FLOP! FLOP!

HERE'S YOUR LUNCH, SONNY BOY!

DON'T WANT IT! I WANT WILD BOAR, NOODLE!

SAYS HE WANTS WILD BOAR WITH NOODLES!

WHAT? WILD BOAR? OH YES, AND WHAT ELSE?!! HE'LL EAT WHAT WE GIVE HIM AND LIKE IT OR LUMP IT!

ALLOW ME TO POINT OUT THAT IF YOUR EXCELLENCY PERSISTS IN REFUSING THIS YOUNG GAUL NOURISHMENT, WE CAN'T COUNT ON RETAINING OUR ONLY BARGAINING COUNTER!

YOU HAVE A POINT. RIGHT! SUMMON MY CHEF GLUTTONUS AND BRING ME THE YOUNG GAUL!

GLUTTONUS IS THE BEST CHEF IN ROME! HE'LL CURE THAT YOUNG BARBARIAN OF HIS BAD TASTE!

FOR STARTERS, I SUGGEST HAWKMOTH CATERPILLARS PRESERVED IN ACACIA HONEY, FOLLOWED BY A PAN OF EARTHWORMS FRIED IN CASTOR OIL. AS THE MAIN DISH, COWS' UDDERS COOKED PLAIN OR IN A SAUCE.

DON'T WANT THAT! WANT WILD BOAR!

!?!?

WE DON'T PIG OUT ON BORING MEAT LIKE THAT IN MY KITCHEN, BY APICIUS!

WANT WILD BOAR!

THE ONLY ONE OF HIS KIND, AND HE HAD TO CROSS MY PATH! GNNNNNNNNNNN!!!

PUT IN AT THE FIRST PORT AND FIND ME A WILD BOAR BEFORE I MAKE HIM SWALLOW...

...WILD BOAR!

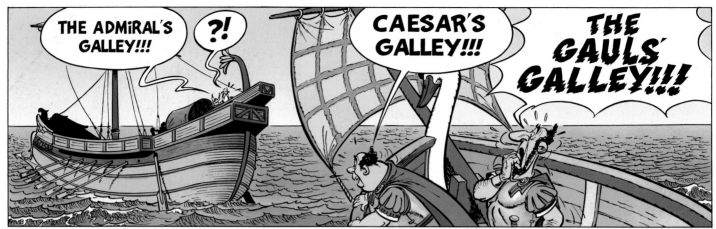

ROMANS, PREPARE TO GET YOUR DESSERTS FOR TAKING A DEFENCELESS CHILD HOSTAGE!

I STILL FIND IT DIFFICULT TO REALIZE IT'S ME HE MEANS!

I HAVE A FEW ACCOUNTS TO SETTLE WITH THESE ROMANS! I WANT THEM TO EAT THE BOILED BOAR THEY TRIED TO STUFF DOWN MY THROAT!

YUK!

YUK!

COME ON, IT'S NOT THAT BAD! IF I ADDED A FEW NICE PLUMP SLUGS MARINATED IN CURRANT JUICE I'M SURE THEY'D GO OVERBOARD FOR IT IN ROME!

HA! HA! HA! HA! HA! HA!

LOOK, WE'VE GONE OVERBOARD HERE AND NOW!

YEAH... YOU WEREN'T GOING TO FORGET US SHIPWRECKED MARINERS, WERE YOU?

COME UP ON BOARD THIS VESSEL, CAP'N! I HAVE A PROPOSITION TO MAKE YOU!

AN HONEST ONE, I HOPE?

BY WAY OF COMPENSATION, WE'LL GIVE YOU JULIUS CAESAR'S GALLEY AND ALL ON BOARD!

WHAT WILL I GET OUT OF THAT?

CAESAR WILL BE SO GLAD TO RECOVER HIS GALLEY, HIS ADMIRAL AND HIS VICE-ADMIRAL, HE'LL PAY YOU ANY RANSOM YOU ASK!

YOU CAN'T DO THIS TO ME!

SHUT UP AND EAT UP!

GIDDY GOAT'S HORNS, LAD, I KNEW WE'D DO BUSINESS SOME DAY! IT'S A BARGAIN! FIFTY-FIFTY, RIGHT?

VERY GENEROUS OF YOU, CAP'N!

SLAP!

GOOD LUCK, CAP'N!

CHEERS, LADDIE!

AND YOU'LL WAIT A LONG TIME TO SEE THE COLOUR OF YOUR FIFTY PERCENT! HO HO HO!

34

THE ADMIRAL'S GALLEY CAPTURED BY THE GAULS IS GOING IN THE OPPOSITE DIRECTION FROM THE GALLEY NOW BEING SAILED BY THE PIRATES.

YOU SAID YOU HAD AN IDEA FOR HELPING OBELIX, O DRUID!

THAT'S RIGHT! IT'S TIME TO TAKE AN IMPORTANT DECISION, ASTERIX!

SPARTAKIS, I BELIEVE YOU'RE A GOOD SAILOR?

SO DO I! I'M GREEK, YOU KNOW!

WOULD YOU AND YOUR CREW AGREE TO TAKE US TO A DISTANT ISLAND?

WHAT'S THIS DISTANT ISLAND CALLED?

ATLANTIS!

?!

?

I THOUGHT THAT LEGENDARY CONTINENT SANK BENEATH THE WAVES LONG AGO!

IT DID. BUT A GROUP OF OFF-SHORE ISLANDS WAS LEFT.* THE LARGEST IS STILL INHABITED BY THE LAST ATLANTEANS!

* SOMETIMES THOUGHT TO BE THE CANARY ISLANDS.

BUT WHAT DOES THIS ATLANTIS PLACE HAVE TO DO WITH OBELIX?

THE ATLANTEANS ARE DESCENDED FROM A VERY ANCIENT CIVILIZATION, FAR MORE ADVANCED THAN OUR OWN. OBELIX COULD BENEFIT FROM THEIR SKILLS!

WE AGREE, DRUID! WE'LL SET COURSE FOR ATLANTIS! ER... THE CREW WOULDN'T MIND BENEFITING FROM YOUR POTION AGAIN.

OF COURSE!

I'LL FETCH SOME FROM THE RESERVE BARREL!

AND THIS LAST BARREL IS FULL OF WATER TOO... BUT THEN... THAT MUST MEAN...

GETAFIX! WE'VE GOT NO MORE MAGIC POTION!

AND THIS TIME YOU CAN'T BLAME ME!

(1) SPAIN
(2) PORTUGAL

37

FOLLOW ME, FRIENDS! COME AND HAVE A LITTLE REST AND REFRESHMENT!

HEY, GETAFIX, LOOK AT THAT! A FLYING COW!!!

WELL, THEY NEED MILK FOR ALL THESE CHILDREN, ASTERIX!

HOW IS IT THAT EXCEPT FOR YOU, HIGH PRIEST, ATLANTIS SEEMS TO BE ENTIRELY INHABITED BY CHILDREN?

ALL THOSE CHILDREN WERE ONCE ADULTS WHO WANTED TO GO BACK TO CHILDHOOD!

YES, I KNOW, THESE ADULTS ARE CR...

IF ONLY THEY AT LEAST HAD FLYING WILD BOAR!!!

GO BACK TO CHILDHOOD? HOW COULD THEY POSSIBLY DO THAT?

OVER MANY CENTURIES THE ATLANTEANS LEARNED AMONG OTHER THINGS, THE SECRET OF REJUVENATION AND ETERNAL YOUTH.

THE SKILLS OF THE ATLANTEANS ARE THE SOLE REASON FOR OUR VOYAGE!

YOU MEAN YOU WANT TO GO BACK TO CHILDHOOD TOO?

NO, QUITE THE OPPOSITE! OBELIX HERE LOST HIS ADULT APPEARANCE BY ACCIDENT. CAN YOU GIVE IT BACK TO HIM?

HE WANTS TO GROW OLDER? THAT'S FUNNY...

UNFORTUNATELY, I KNOW THE SECRET OF THE ELIXIR OF YOUTH BUT NOT THE ELIXIR OF AGE. I'M AFRAID I CAN'T HELP YOUR FRIEND!

OH DEAR! SO WE CAME ALL THIS WAY FOR NOTHING! WE'LL JUST HAVE TO GO HOME TO OUR VILLAGE!

ALL THE SAME, HIGH PRIEST, I MUST SAY I THINK YOUR SKILLS ARE ABSOLUTELY FABULOUS TOO!

I'M ONLY SORRY THEY'RE NO HELP TO YOU!

SOMETIMES I ENVY OUR FRIEND OBELIX! HE DOESN'T KNOW HOW LUCKY HE IS, GETTING HIS CHILDHOOD BACK! WELL, WE'D BETTER BE OFF, THE CREW WILL BE WAITING.

ER... THE FACT IS...

...IF THE HIGH PRIEST AGREES, THE CREW AND I WOULD LIKE TO STAY. ATLANTIS SEEMS TO BE A LAND OF LIBERTY!

!?

?!

VERY WELL, STRICTLY ON CONDITION THAT OUR GAULISH FRIENDS NEVER REVEAL THE EXISTENCE OF ATLANTIS!

WE SWEAR NEVER TO MENTION IT, ABSOLUTLI-FABULOS!

I'M SURE YOU UNDERSTAND, ASTERIX!

OF COURSE! YOU'LL BE REALLY FREE MEN HERE!

I SAY, OLD BOY, WE HAD SOME GOOD TIMES, WHAT?

IT WAS NICE MEETING A LITTLE BUNDLE OF JOY LIKE YOU... AND YOUR SEA-DOG THERE!

CAN WE ASK YOU ONE MORE FAVOUR HIGH PRIEST?

SO NOW WE CAN ONLY RELY ON THE KINDNESS OF AEOLUS* TO GET US HOME.

I THINK I CAN GUESS WHAT IT IS!

I FEAR SO.

* GOD OF THE WINDS.

THE INGREDIENTS FOR THE MAGIC POTION AREN'T AVAILABLE ON THIS ISLAND!

WELL, WE STILL HAVE THE CONTENTS OF MY GOURD IF NECESSARY!

IT'S A SHAME YOU'RE GOING! WE HAVE A GREAT TIME HERE!

40

41

FAR FROM CAESAR'S GALLEY...

ROMAN GALLEY MAKING RIGHT FOR US!

ADMIRAL'S GALLEY RIGHT AHEAD!

THAT'S ODD, I THOUGHT IT WAS MAKING FOR ROME?

WE CAN'T AVOID THEM WITHOUT OARSMEN, ASTERIX!

I STILL HAVE MY GOURD OF MAGIC POTION, REMEMBER?

IT'S THE GAULS!

?!?

THIS IS ODD... LET'S PLAY SAFE AND SEND A WARNING SHOT ACROSS THEIR BOWS BEFORE WE BOARD THEM!

I'M COVERING YOU! DON'T BE AFRAID!

WHO'S AFRAID OF ANYONE?

BE CAREFUL, ASTERIX! I HAVE A NASTY FOREBODING!

GRRRR!

PAF!

SPLOSH

PFFF!

SURRENDER, GAULS!

WHAT HAVE YOU DONE WITH THE ADMIRAL AND HIS CREW? WHO ARE YOU?

YOU'LL SOON FIND OUT IF YOU TOUCH ANOTHER HAIR OF MY FRIEND ASTERIX'S HEAD!

GRRR!

THE SEA HERE IS TEEMING WITH SHARKS... THEY'LL HAVE A FIELD DAY! THROW THIS GAUL WITH THE YELLOW WHISKERS OVERBOARD!

NOOOOO! DON'T DO IT!!! ASTERIX!

ASTERIX!!

WITH A ONE...

GNNNNNN!

?

?

AND A TWO...

GNNNNNN!

GNNNN!

AND A THREE!

I'VE AN IDEA WE'RE GOING TO HAVE FUN AGAIN AT LAST, DOGMATIX!

MUMMY!

WOOF!

AND MY NAME IS OBELIX!

ROW FOR YOUR LIVES!

NO ONE WILL EVER BELIEVE THIS!

PHEW! I FINALLY MANAGED TO SALVAGE THIS GOURD OF...

OBELIX!!! WHAT HAPPENED?

NO IDEA. IT COULD HAVE BEEN THE EFFECT OF SEEING ASTERIX IN DANGER. BUT WHO DID THAT TO YOU... THE ROMANS?

NO, THE SHARKS. BUT I TOOK A MOUTHFUL OF POTION AND THEY DIDN'T PUT THE BITE ON ME!

ASTERIX LOOKS IN BAD SHAPE.

OH. HE'LL SOON BE FINE! A POTION A DAY KEEPS THE ROMANS AWAY!

GLUG! GLUG! GLUG!

?!

OBELIX!!! WHAT HAPPENED?

YES. I KNOW THIS IS GETTING REPETITIVE, BUT IT'S A QUESTION WORTH ASKING!

GOOD THING I BROUGHT YOUR CLOTHES ALONG JUST IN CASE!

YOU'RE THE BEST FRIEND I KNOW, ASTERIX!

AAAAH! IT'S GOOD TO GET BACK TO MY OWN SIZE!

AND IT'LL BE GOOD TO GET HOME! HIGH TIME WE WENT BACK TO THE VILLAGE!

DOGMATIX AND I WILL ROW!

YIPPEE!!

MEANWHILE, FAR AWAY...

THE ADMIRAL'S BEEN DOWN THERE AN AWFULLY LONG TIME! I'D BETTER TAKE A LOOK!

?!

WHAT THE... HE'S TURNED TO STONE!!!

TAP! TAP! TAP!

THIS MUST BE THE HARDEST WATER EVER!

BUT... BUT NOW I CAN TAKE CAESAR HIS GALLEY BACK ON MY OWN! HE'LL PROMOTE ME TO ADMIRAL AT LEAST!

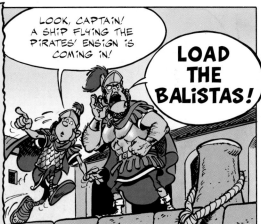

HOWEVER... AT THIS MOMENT A YOUNG OFFICER AND A CAPTAIN WITHOUT A SHIP ARE ON DUTY IN CHARGE OF THE SECURITY OF OSTIA, THE PORT OF ROME.

LOOK, CAPTAIN! A SHIP FLYING THE PIRATES' ENSIGN IS COMING IN!

LOAD THE BALISTAS!

WHEN I GIVE THE WORD...

FIRE!

SWOOSH!

?!

CRASH!

CAVE CAESAR

LET'S BE MAGNANIMOUS AND PICK UP THOSE STUPID, IMPUDENT AND PRETENTIOUS PIRATES!

WHY... WHY, IT'S YOU, VICE ADMIRAL NAUTILUS!

SO IT IS! AND IF YOU WANT TO SEE THE ADMIRAL, HE'S DOWN BELOW!

?

SO STATUES ARE WEARING CLOTHES NOW?

IT'S THE DECADENT LATE ROMAN STYLE!

THIS IS A DISASTER! JULIUS CAESAR'S OWN GALLEY!!!

YES, AND WHICH OF US IS GOING TO TELL HIM ABOUT IT?

NOT VERY FAR FROM HOME NOW, OBELIX!

YOU KNOW, I'D LIKE TO MAKE A LITTLE DETOUR BEFORE WE REACH THE VILLAGE, ASTERIX!

I'VE AN IDEA OBELIX WANTS TO PAY THE CAMP OF AQUARIUM A VISIT.

WELL, WE OWE HIM SOME FUN!

ADMIRAL'S GALLEY IN SIGHT!

HUH! YET ANOTHER BRASS HAT!

WHAT... WHAT ARE THEY DOING?

SNOOZING, YOU BET!

RAISE THE....

THE END

UDERZO - 96